Understanding AWS WAF and Shield False Positives

Table of Contents

Chapter 1. Introduction

Special Report: Navigating the Maze of AWS WAF and Shield False Positives

In an era fueled by innovative technology, no one can afford to lag behind, especially when it pertains to cloud-based security solutions like Amazon Web Services (AWS) Web Application Firewall (WAF) and AWS Shield. Welcome to our special report that delves into the realm of these protective services, and walks you comprehensively through the intricacies of false positives. Understanding false positives, their causes, and methods to reduce them is pivotal in optimizing the security posture of any organization. Presented in an approachable, down-to-earth manner, this report aims to illuminate this highly technical subject, making it manageable and practicable even for the non-tech enthusiasts amongst us. Don't be resident of the shadows; step into the light of understanding with this must-have guide to AWS WAF and Shield False Positives.

Chapter 2. Understanding AWS WAF and AWS Shield: An Overview

As we delve into the complex realm of AWS WAF and AWS Shield, it's important to ground ourselves with a solid understanding of these two services, their functions, characteristics and how they interact in the broader AWS ecosystem. In this chapter, we will be laying the groundwork for your holistic understanding of these two core components of AWS' security suite, defining key terms, and explaining some of the fundamental principles that drive these technologies.

2.1. AWS Web Application Firewall (WAF)

At its core, the AWS Web Application Firewall is a security tool designed to protect your applications by filtering and monitoring HTTP/HTTPS traffic between AWS resources and the Internet. WAF acts as a fortress gate, enabling you to control the traffic that reaches your applications and block common web exploits like SQL injection and XSS (Cross-Site Scripting).

WAF functions using conditions, rules, and rule groups that inspect web requests. Conditions define what to look for in a request (namely IPs, HTTP headers, HTTP methods, URI strings, SQL injection and XSS). Rules use conditions to identify potential threat patterns, while rule groups are simply a collection of rules.

When a web request matches the conditions in a rule, AWS WAF can perform one of three actions: allow the request, block the request or count (monitor) the request. The way AWS WAF responds to a matched condition is crucial in identifying and managing false positives.

2.2. AWS Shield

While WAF is proficient in addressing common vulnerabilities encountered in web applications, AWS Shield is particularly adept at mitigating one specific type of attack - Distributed Denial of Service (DDoS). AWS Shield is a managed DDoS protection service safeguarding applications on AWS.

There are two tiers to AWS Shield: Standard and Advanced. Every AWS customer receives the benefits of Shield Standard, providing protection against most common and frequently observed DDoS attacks. However, Shield Advanced offers costlier, more comprehensive protection, targeting larger and more sophisticated DDoS attacks. Additionally, it provides cost protection, web application firewall integration, DDoS cost protection, and 24/7 DDoS response team (DRT) access.

It's important to note that AWS Shield works in tandem with AWS WAF, supplementing its capabilities rather than replacing it.

2.3. Integration of AWS WAF and AWS Shield

AWS WAF and AWS Shield are designed to work in harmony, providing an encompassing security envelope for AWS-hosted applications. While WAF offers detailed protection against application layer exploits, Shield fortifies defenses against volumetric, state-exhaustion and reflection attacks that aim at the network and transport layers.

Moreover, AWS Shield Advanced includes integration with AWS WAF at no extra cost. Through this integration, AWS Shield can feed information about ongoing DDoS attacks to AWS WAF, which can adjust its rules to better block malicious traffic. This results in a dynamic, adaptable defense solution capable of responding to complex and evolving threats.

2.4. The AWS Ecosystem and Cloud Security

Neither AWS Shield nor WAF exist in a vacuum - they are integral parts of a larger AWS security architecture. The AWS ecosystem offers numerous other services that complement and enhance WAF and Shield. These include services like Route 53 (for DNS), CloudFront (for content delivery), and many others. Essentially, the WAF and Shield provide pieces of a holistic cloud security strategy employing a network of diverse, interconnected services.

Cloud security should never be understood solely through the lens of isolated tools like WAF or Shield. Instead, successful security strategies view these services within the broader AWS landscape and consider how they can be utilized in tandem with other security features to create a comprehensive defense against the vast spectrum of cybersecurity threats.

In later chapters, we will dive deeper into the finer mechanics of AWS WAF, delve further into AWS Shield's DDoS protection capabilities, and finally, explore how to navigate the maze of false positives inherent in any powerful security suite. The knowledge you glean from this chapter will serve as a stepping stone to understanding AWS WAF's and Shield's functioning and how to fine-tune their settings to enhance your security posture while minimizing false positives.

Chapter 3. Cracking the Code: False Positives Explained

In any endeavor to promote security standards and practices, clarity is crucial, and to that end, let us demystify the concept of false positives in the realm of AWS WAF and Shield.

For starters, when we talk about false positives, we are referring to an event that is incorrectly identified as a threat by a security system. In this case, AWS WAF or Shield identifies a legitimate application or system behavior as suspicious, warranting a security alert or even blocking the action.

3.1. The Origin of False Positives

The formulation of false positives hinges on how security systems like AWS WAF and Shield interpret the behavior against a set of predefined rules or definitions that determine what is deemed 'normal' or 'abnormal.' AWS WAF, an ingenuously designed protective shield, uses what are known as 'rules' to delineate malicious activity. Similarly, AWS Shield leverages preconfigured protective features that can inadvertently mark legitimate activity as a threat. By understanding this genesis, we can better govern these services, maximize their efficiency, and significantly reduce the occurrence of false positives.

False positives can originate from a variety of circumstances, including misconfigured settings, overly broad rule definitions, rapidly evolving attack vectors, and the dynamic nature of applications. It's also noteworthy that ongoing updates and modifications to applications can unintentionally trigger security rules, leading to false positives.

3.2. The Implications of False Positives

The implications of false positives extend beyond mere annoyance. They hold far-reaching consequences for any organization. The excessive flood of false positives can inundate security teams, distracting them from identifying and addressing real threats. This might also lead to an ominous sense of "alert fatigue", where critical alerts might go unnoticed. In severe cases, false positives can interrupt or block legitimate transactions or operations, leading to lost revenue, productivity, or even reputational damage.

However grim it may sound, the issue of false positives is not beyond the realm of control. They can be managed and even significantly reduced by comprehending the design and functionality of AWS WAF and Shield and implementing strategic best practices.

3.3. AWS WAF and False Positives

To curb the flurry of false positives, it's crucial to understand how AWS WAF functions. AWS WAF works on a set of rules, with each rule containing a set of conditions that inspect web requests. If a request matches these conditions, AWS WAF counts the request as a match or in some configurations, it can block the request.

You configure AWS WAF by creating WebACLs that contain rules, where a rule contains one or more statements that look for specific strings, SQL injections, scripts, and such. When you add a rule to a WebACL, you define an action for each rule, which could be 'Block', 'Allow', or 'Count'.

The 'Block' will block requests, the 'Allow' will allow the requests and the 'Count' action simply counts requests that match the conditions in the rule. In this case, even though the 'Count' action does not block requests, it can still flag false positives if the rule conditions are too broad or misconfigured.

3.4. AWS Shield and False Positives

AWS Shield operates at a slightly different tangent. It's a managed DDoS protection service that defends applications running on AWS. AWS Shield provides automatic application scaling to absorb DDoS attacks, and also provides DDoS cost protection for higher scale DDoS events.

Here, too, the problem of false positives can occur. Because of the broad protection AWS Shield offers, sometimes normal spikes in traffic or application behavior might be identified as abnormal and potentially harmful. This leads to false positives that can block legitimate requests.

3.5. Best Practices to Handle False Positives

Now that we have comprehended the workings of AWS WAF and AWS Shield and how false positives spring up, let's identify some best practices that can serve to reduce and manage these false positives effectively.

* Fine-tune rule configurations: Misconfigured rules or conditions can lead to a surge in false positives. Invest time to understand your applications' normal behavior, and tailor your rules to suit this behavior. Be mindful not to cast the rules too wide. This might involve time and research, but will ultimately lead to a reduction in false positives.

* Leverage 'Count' Action: Use the 'Count' action judiciously in AWS WAF. This action allows you to test and validate your rules without blocking wanted traffic. Once sure of the rule correctness, you can switch the action to 'Block' or 'Allow'.

* Constant review and improvement: Regularly reviewing your AWS WAF and Shield settings can help nip the problem of false positives in the bud. Be open to iterations and improvements and consider refining rules as per evolving application behavior and developing threat scenarios.

* Intelligent alerting: Instead of blasting your security team with every single alert, consider intelligent alerting that prioritizes alerts based on severity and frequency. This can help prevent alert fatigue and ensure that actual threats do not go undetected.

The journey of understanding, confronting, and addressing false positives with AWS WAF and Shield might seem daunting. Yet, with a persistent pursuit of knowledge, regular review of rules and conditions, coupled with the smart application of best practices, we can significantly mitigate the impact of false positives. As we continue to harness the power of AWS WAF and Shield, let us also remember to skillfully navigate the course between high security and functional flexibility.

Chapter 4. Causative Factors Behind AWS WAF and Shield False Positives

Web Application Firewalls (WAFs) and protective tools like AWS Shield are robust security measures designed to protect applications and data from a variety of attacks. Nothing, however, comes without its caveats, false positives being one of them. By understanding the various causative factors, we can take steps to manage false positives efficiently.

4.1. Network Configuration Errors

Network configuration errors are one of the common causes of false positives. If the firewall interprets your network setup incorrectly, it could identify legitimate traffic as an attack, leading to false positives. This can occur due to incorrect security group configurations or misconfigurations in ingress or egress rules.

Amending erroneous configurations will invariably aid in reducing these. It is crucial to check the configurations thoroughly for any anomalies and to correct them promptly to mitigate the risk of false positives. AWS provides documentation and resources to guide users through the correct processes of network configuration.

4.2. Inappropriate Security Rules

Another common cause of false positives is inappropriate security rules. Rules that are not accurately defined can flag legitimate requests as threats. For instance, the enforcement rule could be excessively restrictive, yielding a higher instance of false positives than necessary.

To mitigate this, a thorough review of the applied rules is essential. For instance, in AWS WAF, the use of preconfigured Managed Rules can assist in defining superior parameters, thereby minimizing the risk of inappropriate rules leading to false positives. It is also beneficial to review these rules regularly to ensure they are fine-tuned to suit the application's evolving needs.

4.3. Changes in Network Traffic Patterns

Changes in network traffic patterns could also trigger false positives. AWS WAF and Shield are designed to learn from the incoming traffic and adjust their defense mechanism accordingly. However, an abrupt change in the traffic pattern could be seen as an anomaly and lead to regular traffic being flagged.

Benchmarking normal traffic vs. expected traffic can provide a reference point for identifying anomalies. This approach also aids in reducing the system's sensitivity to minor fluctuations in traffic. Regular monitoring of traffic patterns and adjustments of policies to suit these shifts can assist in reducing the rate of false positives.

4.4. High Sensitivity to Attacks

A highly reactive WAF and Shield could lead to a significant number of false positives. A highly sensitive defense mechanism may recognize legitimate requests to be a threat due to similar characteristics or patterns.

To manage this, it is essential to set security policies on AWS WAF and Shield at an optimum level. Regular tuning of the sensitivity level to suit your data traffic and applications can reduce the instances of false positives significantly.

4.5. Misclassification due to Pattern Detection

False positives are sometimes the result of misclassification due to pattern detection. AWS WAF and Shield use pattern detection to identify potential threats. Occasionally, these patterns may overlap with legitimate operations, causing them to be flagged.

To mitigate, constant monitoring and tuning of the detection system is necessary to ensure legitimate patterns of operation aren't inadvertently flagged. A thorough understanding of how pattern detection works in AWS WAF and AWS Shield can greatly assist in managing this issue.

4.6. Incomplete or Incorrectly Categorized IP Reputation Lists

AWS WAF employs IP reputation lists to block or allow requests. Errors in these lists, such as out-of-date IP addresses or incorrectly categorized IPs, can generate an unanticipated number of false positives. Regular updates and meticulous management of these lists are essential in maintaining their effectiveness and integrity.

In conclusion, managing false positives in AWS WAF and Shield is about understanding the system's nature and the factors leading to false positives. Familiarity with your application, traffic patterns, and how your firewall interprets them offers a good foundation for managing false positives. Regular monitoring, tuning, and education can reduce unnecessary alerts, ensuring your security setup is as effective and efficient as possible.

Chapter 5. The Blueprint of AWS WAF: An In-depth Analysis

AWS WAF, standing for Web Application Firewall, is a security service that aids in protecting your web applications or APIs against standard web exploits that might otherwise affect application availability and security, or consume excessive resources.

The operation of AWS WAF lies in allowing or blocking HTTP(S) requests to and from web applications based on specific conditions that align with your security strategy. These conditions also known as 'rules,' encompass components like IP addresses, HTTP headers, HTTP body, URI strings, SQL injection patterns, and Cross-site Scripting (XSS) attacks.

5.1. Functionality of AWS WAF

AWS WAF provides a set of customizable security factors. These involve rule assignments that permit, block, or monitor (count) web requests based upon predetermined aspects like sources of IP addresses or match conditions that draw on identifiers like SQL code or harmful scripts.

The stipulated conditions are carefully organized into Rule statements, Rule groups, and WebACLs.

Rule statements: A rule statement is the primary building block. It identifies patterns and marks the foundation for AWS WAF's decision-making process. It specifies what needs to be identified (like IP addresses or SQL code) and the action upon detection (allow, block, or count).

Rule groups: As the name suggests, rule groups are simply a collection of several rule statements assembled into a single set. It can be reused across multiple AWS applications and resources. For instance, organizations can define a rule group to prevent any region-specific IP ranges from access.

WebACLs: Standing for Access Control List, WebACL is the foremost decision-making unit of the AWS WAF. It allows or denies access to AWS resources after scrutinizing the requested traffic against all the rule statements and rule groups that fall under its structure.

5.2. AWS WAF: Rooted in Rules

In AWS WAF, rules are the foundational elements that guard your applications. Everything from identifying malicious activity, taking countermeasures, or even just counting suspicious requests, rules are at the forefront.

An individual rule within AWS WAF includes a set of match conditions and actions, and are flexible and customisable. You can choose from several predefined protective features (like SQL injection prevention or cross-site scripting (XSS) protection), or tailor-make a rule to meet your unique requirements.

There are three types of rules available in AWS WAF:

. Regular rules: These are your run-of-the-mill rules that contain a set of conditions that AWS WAF searches for in incoming web requests.

. Rate-based rules: These rules act like a defensive barrier against potential DDoS attacks or brute force login attempts. They function by limiting the number of web requests from an IP address per chosen time frame.

. Rule groups: These are not individual rules, per se. Instead, they are a collection of regular and rate-based rules grouped together. Rule groups have a dual purpose. They allow more systematic rule management, and AWS provides managed rule groups, maintained and updated by AWS security experts.

5.3. In the Mind of AWS WAF: The Decision-making Process

Now that you are acquainted with the elements comprising AWS WAF, let's dive into how they work collectively, harmonizing into a robust defense mechanism.

Once a web request reaches AWS WAF, it first runs through all the specified WebACL's rules in the order they've been defined. The rule that gets the first match dictates the action, which can either be 'allow', 'block', or 'count'. If no rules match, AWS WAF takes the default action.

1. If a web request matches an 'Allow' rule statement, AWS WAF allows the request through.

2. If a web request meets a 'Block' rule, AWS WAF blocks the request outright.

3. If a rule with 'Count' is matched, the request is allowed to pass, but the event is logged for future analysis.

This process ensures a rapid response that minimally disturbs the normal flow of the web traffic, even while actively safeguarding your resources.

5.4. A Rundown on Creating and Managing AWS WAF Rules

Getting started with AWS WAF requires defining your rules. This endeavor, while primarily astute, can also be efficiently streamlined for your convenience using AWS Management Console, AWS WAF APIs, AWS SDKs, or AWS CLI.

The following steps detail the general overview of rule creation:

1. Access AWS WAF either via the AWS Management Console, AWS WAF APIs, AWS SDKs, or AWS CLI.

2. Create a new Rule or Rule Group.

3. Specify the conditions for your rule. Decide what you want AWS WAF to look for.

4. Choose an action for your rule. This can be 'Allow', 'Block', or 'Count'.

5. Integrate your rule into a WebACL and set up the inspection order.

6. Apply the WebACL to an AWS resource.

After the successful initialization of the rules, AWS WAF begins inspecting incoming web requests according to the stipulated conditions.

5.5. Advanced Features of AWS WAF

While exploring the blueprint of AWS WAF, it's worth noting its specialized features that add further resilience to your web application security. Let's go through them.

. Managed Rule Groups: AWS Managed Rule Groups are a curated set of pre-configured rules that address common security issues. Regularly updated by AWS security experts, they provide an accessible route to securing your applications without needing advanced expertise.

. AWS WAF Capacity Units: AWS WAF employs a system of Capacity

Units (WCUs) to handle the resources needed for handling your rules. Each rule statement assigned to a web ACL uses a specific number of WCUs, providing a consistent way of managing your AWS WAF service.

. Logging and monitoring: AWS WAF provides robust logging and monitoring services to keep an eye on your security cover's health. It integrates with Amazon CloudWatch, allowing you to set alarms for specific trigger points. Integration with AWS Kinesis Data Firehose allows for extensive query and analysis options.

By diving into the blueprint of AWS WAF, organizations can appreciate the service's layered and customizable defense mechanism. Whether it involves screening IP addresses, scrutinizing HTTP Requests, or preventing SQL or Cross-Site Scripting attacks, AWS WAF is a formidable security champion, navigating the risky cyber landscape and proactively ensuring threat mitigation. However, it also introduces the challenge of 'false positives,' wherein legitimate requests are incorrectly flagged as harmful. This report will continue with exploring how to understand, manage, and reduce these false positives for optimal security performance.

Chapter 6. Diving Deeper into AWS Shield: A Comprehensive Breakdown

AWS Shield, a part of Amazon Web Services, is an intricate fortress of instruments designed to protect web applications from Distributed Denial of Service (DDoS) attacks. Its system architecture diffuses nefarious packets, mitigates application vulnerabilities, and reinforces the defences of your servers. AWS Shield fits snugly into the safety ecosystem, providing advanced shielding in addition to the baseline security offered by the AWS WAF.

6.1. Understanding AWS Shield

In essence, AWS Shield is a Managed DDoS protection service that safeguards applications hosted within the AWS expanse. Available in two tiers, AWS Shield Standard and AWS Shield Advanced, it provides disparate levels of protection. From the standard level designed to protect against most common DDoS attacks to the Advanced level intended to deter larger, more complex attacks---users can choose a service tier that corresponds with their circumstance and budget.

Shield Standard automatically protects all AWS customers at no additional charge. It offers defence against the majority of frequently seen DDoS attacks that could imperil application availability. Contrarily, Shield Advanced provides advanced DDoS mitigation capabilities against larger and sophisticated attacks, cost protection, and 24/7 DDoS response team (DRT) access.

6.2. Differentiating AWS Shield Standard from AWS Shield Advanced

Shield Standard, enhancing the built-in protections of AWS's services, endeavours to safeguard your applications from the common, most frequently observed DDoS attacks. It fears no additional cost, hence providing an entry point for small businesses or those with less security demands.

Shield Advanced, aimed primarily at higher risk applications, provides higher level of DDoS protection. Included within its remit are features like Cost Protection (which covers extra data transfer costs), 24/7 DDoS response team access, proactive application threat intelligence, and advanced threat protection. While it carries an additional cost, its benefits outweigh the expenditure for organizations dealing with high-value data or larger attack surfaces.

6.3. Addressing Typically Encountered DDoS Attack Types

Shield's main task is to fend off DDoS attacks. These attacks aim to overload a network, service, or server with superfluous requests to exhaust resources and bandwidth, thereby slowing down service or causing complete unavailability for legitimate users. Few of the commonly observed attack types include:

- UDP Reflection Attacks

- SYN Flood

- HTTP Flood

- SQL Injection

- DNS Query Flood

Shield splits these attacks into three categories for mitigation—
Infrastructure Layer (Layer 3 and Layer 4), State Exhaustion attacks,
and Application Layer (Layer 7).

6.4. The Synergy Between AWS Shield and AWS WAF

To deliver a robust, holistic security solution, Shield works in tandem
with AWS WAF. While Shield focuses on DDoS protection, WAF
targets more convoluted threats such as SQL injection and Cross Site
Scripting (XSS). This combo serves to stave off a broad array of
application level attacks, making it an encompassing solution to
address most security concerns for web applications hosted on AWS
ecosystem.

6.5. Managing AWS Shield Advanced

Management of Shield Advanced is facilitated by AWS Management
Console, AWS CLI, or AWS SDKs. Shield Advanced gives you an
intuitive dashboard to help understand the ongoing security posture
of your applications. It provides vital statistics, threat assessment,
and recommendations for action.

6.6. Deciphering the Financial Aspects

Shield Advanced, being a premium service, comes with its own costs.
However, this service is a boon in times of crises. In the wake of a
DDoS attack, this doesn't only offer protection but also ensures cost
protection, meaning that it covers the extra costs incurred due to the
enhanced data transfer caused by the attack.

Shield provides robust application defense without the complexity, creating a user-friendly environment for businesses to safely operate. Its synergy with existing AWS services and updated features to address evolving risks ensures that AWS Shield remains a compelling offering in the field of web application protection.

-End of Comprehensive Breakdown-

Chapter 7. Navigating the Maze of AWS WAF and Shield Configurations

The introduction of Amazon Web Services (AWS) into the realm of cloud security, specifically AWS Web Application Firewall (WAF) and AWS Shield, has undeniably bolstered its efficiency. Yet, this complex landscape can often feel like a labyrinth, a woven tapestry of configurations that can easily confuse even the most technically endowed users. Allow us to be your guide as we navigate this labyrinth, going under the hood of AWS WAF and AWS Shield configurations.

7.1. AWS WAF Architectural Understanding

The AWS WAF is a flexible and customizable web application firewall. Its primary role is to safeguard your applications by inspecting the HTTP and HTTPS traffic directed towards them. To begin grasping the complexity involved, let's dive into the architecture.

Within the AWS WAF framework exist 'rules' that allow or block web traffic to your servers. The decision to allow or block is conditional, governed by certain criteria including IP addresses, HTTP headers, HTTP body, SSL/TLS certificate parameters, query string, and URI paths. You store each rule inside a 'WebACL' to further customize your controls, effectively creating a defensive wall around your web applications.

Each 'WebACL' consists of a default action ("allow all" or "block all") and a priority-organized set of rules. AWS WAF evaluates these rules based on their priority hierarchy, from the high to lower, stopping once a rule is triggered.

7.2. AWS Shield Configurations

The purpose of AWS Shield is to ensure advanced protection to your applications against large and sophisticated Distributed Denial of Service (DDoS) attacks. Available in two tiers, AWS Shield Standard protects against most common DDoS attacks, and is included with AWS at no additional cost. For higher level security, AWS Shield Advanced offers protection against larger and more sophisticated attacks, at an additional cost and with DDoS cost protection.

7.3. Deeper into Configurations: Singling out the AWS WAF Rules

Let's turn our attention to AWS WAF rules. Understanding the possible rules that you can create to enhance your defenses can be a real game-changer. There are three types of rules:

1. Regular rules are the standard set that use basic string matching and are evaluated in order.

2. Rate-based rules allow you to restrict traffic from IP addresses once they cross a specified 'rate limit'. Useful in preventing brute force attacks.

3. Group rules enable businesses to organize and enforce sets of shared rules across various applications/services.

Another intricate facet of AWS WAF configurations is the use of 'rule actions', that will instruct AWS WAF on the rule trigger:

- 'Allow' action will permit the requests that match rule specifications.

- 'Block' action will not allow these requests.

- 'Count' action will merely record them in a dashboard.

7.4. The Maze of AWS Shield Advanced

AWS Shield Advanced offers a further configuration maze, directly integrated with AWS WAF, to provide another layer to your cybersecurity architecture.

In the AWS Shield Advanced service, 'DDoS protection groups' or 'composite alarms' are particularly noteworthy. They allow you to group AWS resources for collective DDoS threat monitoring and protection. It employs Amazon CloudWatch alarms to notify you promptly of potential threats.

7.5. Orchestrating AWS WAF and AWS Shield

Now that we have unveiled the individual components of AWS WAF and Shield services, we can explore their orchestration. Taking advantage of this complementary integration brings another level of precision to your application's security.

Remember that AWS WAF protects at an application level, filtering traffic that exposes vulnerabilities in your code. Meanwhile, AWS Shield safeguards infrastructure by absorbing and deflecting volumetric DDoS attacks. The combination allows you to devise fine-grained, layered defensive tactics for encompassing protection.

7.6. Wrapping up with AWS Firewall Manager

The AWS Firewall Manager adds the final touch, managing your WAF and Shield configurations across accounts and applications. It allows security admins to centrally control their security profile, ensuring consistent application of security layers across the board. It also reduces administrative burden, providing much-needed simplicity amidst configuration complexity.

AWS Firewall Manager also supports 'policies', each associated with a specific WAF 'rule group' or Shield 'protection group'. This lets you replicate successful protective rules across the mass of AWS resources, optimizing your defense posture.

Cracking the code of AWS WAF and Shield configurations might seem like a convoluted task. But by understanding their architectural designs and the relationships between their components, you can master your cloud security strategies, steering through this technological labyrinth with newfound confidence.

Chapter 8. Isolating and Mitigating False Positives in AWS WAF

Before diving into the practical techniques for isolating and mitigating false positives within AWS WAF (Web Application Firewall), it's crucial to have at least a rudimentary understanding of what constitutes a 'false positive'. Simply put, a false positive occurs when the WAF mistakenly identifies legitimate traffic or actions as threats. The complexity of modern web applications and their myriad interactions often lead to these misidentifications. The unfortunate byproduct of this issue can be blocked or hindered access to essential services for perfectly valid users - a situation no organization wants. Therefore, the correct identification and mitigation of false positives become crucial for an optimal user experience, while effectively maintaining robust security.

8.1. Understanding AWS WAF and Its Rules

AWS WAF functions based on a set of preconfigured or custom rules aimed at identifying and blocking potentially harmful web traffic. These rules are specific conditions or thresholds that help in detecting possible threats, such as SQL injections or cross-site scripting (XSS) attacks. The way WAF works, by default, is denying anything that's not explicitly permitted. Therefore, any request that inadvertently hits one of these rules is flagged and may consequently be blocked - a key source of false positives. It's helpful to regularly review and adapt these rules, thereby ensuring they continue to serve their role effectively, without hindering genuine traffic.

8.2. AWS WAF Logging: Your First Step Towards Isolation

The most practical starting point in isolating false positives is using AWS WAF Logs. AWS WAF provides comprehensive logging capabilities that record all the traffic inspected by the firewall, including allowed and blocked requests based on corresponding rules. These logs are beneficial for understanding the source, nature, and pattern of requests, providing crucial insights into your web application's interaction with various traffic.

AWS WAF logs are stored in Amazon S3 buckets, formatted as JSON objects. These logs include detailed information about the request - HTTP method, headers, client IP, URI, the rule that acted upon the request, and more. Analyzing these logs is your golden key to spotting patterns that might lead to false positives. Note: it's essential to enable logging in your AWS WAF settings for this to work.

8.3. Leveraging Amazon CloudWatch for False Positive Identification

With AWS WAF logs in hand, one powerful tool for their analysis is Amazon CloudWatch. Not only can it handle the volume of data in the logs, but it also gives you the ability to create custom dashboards and reports based upon your particular needs. Alerts can also be set up to provide real-time notifications about spikes in blocked requests that might indicate a problem.

By setting up metrics within CloudWatch based on the information from AWS WAF logs, users can isolate false positives over a period of time. For instance, tracking the number of times a specific rule has acted upon can help identify its overactivity and the tendency to flag valid requests.

8.4. Tackling False Positives: AWS WAF Rule Tuning and Custom Rules

Once false positives have been identified, the next step is mitigating them. A practical way is to adjust your AWS WAF rules. Rule fine-tuning involves adjusting the conditions of the troublesome rules causing the false positives. This could potentially involve modifying an IP set in a rule, tweaking a rate-based rule's limit, or even changing a string match condition.

It's worth noting that while adjusting and fine-tuning preconfigured rules serve as effective preliminary steps, the creation of custom rules for AWS WAF offers the most flexibility and precision in reducing false positives. Custom rules are designed specifically around your application's unique patterns and nature, offering a higher level of granularity and control. They allow you to tailor how AWS WAF responds to particular conditions, helping you balance stringent security while minimizing false positives.

Additionally, AWS Managed Rules offer a set of pre-built rules created by AWS's security team. These rules cover common threat categories and can be fine-tuned to better fit your web application's profile.

8.5. Regular Auditing and Review

Regular auditing and review of your AWS WAF rule performance is crucial to maintaining a low rate of false positives. This includes keeping a close watch on CloudWatch metrics, regularly scrutinizing AWS WAF logs, and continuously tweaking rule parameters to align with the ever-changing landscape of web applications and user interaction patterns.

In conclusion, dealing with the mammalian task of isolating and mitigating false positives with AWS WAF requires a sound knowledge of your web application's behavior, robust data analysis skills, and a continuous-improvement mindset. Remember, the goal isn't to eliminate false positives - an impossible task, considering the evolving nature of threats - but to reduce their occurrence to a minimum, facilitating a seamless user experience while maintaining uncompromising security.

Chapter 9. Recipe for Success: Reducing False Positives in AWS Shield

Enhancing the effectiveness of AWS Shield involves honing detection mechanisms to reduce false positives. These unwanted alerts can affect productivity and compromise security by causing unnecessary diversions.

9.1. Understanding False Positives

False positives in AWS Shield or any other Protective Distributed Denial of Service (DDoS) mechanisms can be described as legitimate traffic being flagged as malicious. This occurs due to the anomaly detection algorithms within the system, which may erroneously classify standard activities as potential threats. Such instances can lead to inefficiencies within the system and exhaust resources that could be better utilized.

The dangers of excessive false positives include causing alarm fatigue, essentially desensitizing your security team to alarm events over time, even rendering them dismissive of potential threats due to the frequency of false alarms. This could lead to legitimate threats being overlooked, causing harm to the system.

9.2. Fine-Tuning Detection Mechanisms

The pivot of improving AWS Shield efficiency lies in the fine-tuning of detection mechanisms. To minimize false positives, it's critical to adjust these mechanisms to better differentiate between benign and potentially harmful activities, usually achieved through machine learning techniques.

Chapter 10. Anomaly Detection Algorithms

Anomaly detection is the process by which unusual patterns or behaviours are identified within a system. In the case of AWS Shield, these algorithms are employed to detect unusual traffic patterns that may be indicative of a DDoS attack. The primary challenge lies in distinguishing between anomalous traffic with malicious intent and that which is simply unusual yet benign activity.

Machine learning comes into play here. You can deploy machine learning models to learn the 'normal' behaviour of your system's traffic. The better the model's understanding of the standard activity, the higher its accuracy in distinguishing malicious patterns.

Chapter 11. Tuning Anomaly Detection Parameters

The settings of your anomaly detection system can significantly impact the rate of false positives. The sensitivity of the system is typically adjustable, allowing for a more precise tuning based on your traffic pattern's specific characteristics.

Typically, a high sensitivity setting will catch more potential threats but may lead to a higher rate of false positives. Conversely, lower sensitivity may result in fewer false positives but could potentially let real threats slip through. This is a delicate balance that should be tailored to your specific traffic patterns and risk tolerance.

11.1. Dealing With Known Legitimate Traffic

In some cases, you may experience a recurring false positive concerning certain IP addresses or specific sequences of activities that continue to be flagged due to the system's security settings.

In such scenarios, it is advisable to manually validate these activities as benign and create exceptions within your detection system. Remember, though, any exception provided should be reviewed periodically to ascertain that these activities remain benign over time.

11.2. Employing Rate-Based Rules

AWS Shield allows the use of Rate-Based Rules (RBRs), which are primarily designed to protect against volumetric attacks. RBRs function by counting the requests from each IP address to any AWS resource. When this count exceeds a predefined threshold, additional mitigation measures come into effect.

While RBRs can be powerful tools in preventing DDoS attacks, be advised that improper tuning can lead to high rates of false positives. As such, a keen understanding of your regular traffic patterns is paramount to maximize the effectiveness of RBRs.

11.3. Collaborative Approach to Security

Security measures, including AWS Shield, do not exist in a vacuum and are made most effective when employed as part of an integrated and holistic security strategy. When AWS Shield protection is used in conjunction with other security measures like AWS WAF, the likelihood of false positives can be significantly reduced, as multiple detection mechanisms are in play concurrently.

11.4. Regular Reviews and Continuous Improvement

Reducing false positives is not a one-off exercise but a continuous process. Regularly reviewing your security processes and threat detection mechanisms can help identify any tweaks necessary to minimize false positives. Leveraging AWS's regular updates and incorporating feedback from the security team can be valuable in maintaining an optimized balance between detection and avoidance of false positives.

The process of minimizing false positives in any security infrastructure is an ongoing task, requiring attention, analysis, and often, fine-tuning. With the right understanding, process review and continuous learning, AWS Shield could serve as a robust defensive tool, shielding your applications from DDoS attacks while keeping false positives to a minimum.

Chapter 12. Case Study: Real-world Scenarios of False Positive Management

Understanding false positives within the scope of AWS WAF and Shield begins with real-world applications. As such, this comprehensive case study aims to offer a handful of examples to illustrate the management of false positives.

12.1. Scenario One: E-commerce Business

Let's start with a common example. An e-commerce business relies heavily on its website for its day-to-day operations. Its security setup includes AWS WAF and AWS Shield, configured with a set of custom rules to prevent attacks.

In one instance, a high frequency of requests from a particular IP address triggered a rule, thus causing the WAF to drop the requests from that IP. However, it turned out these were legitimate requests from a loyal customer trying to purchase goods in bulk during a sale. This is a classic case of false positive, a legitimate action being flagged as malicious.

The solution is to refine the WAF rules. Rule conditions can be amended to consider frequency within a certain period from the same IP address, as well as to regard known customer IP addresses in an allow list. Continuous monitoring and refining of the WAF rules helped reduce such false positives, enhancing user experience without compromising security.

12.2. Scenario Two: Public Voting System

Shifting the lens to another sector, we examine a public voting system for an online contest. To prevent fraudulent votes, they employ AWS WAF and Shield as part of their security measures.

During peak voting periods, a large number of requests, often from similar IP ranges, flood the website. The WAF flags these as potential DDoS attacks, causing numerous legitimate votes to be lost. Another case of a false positive that significantly impacts the running of the contest.

The response to this involves a multi-faceted approach. To differentiate between DDoS attacks and genuine voting traffic spikes, the system administrators need to adjust the threshold parameters for rate-based rules in the WAF. Besides, they also consider implementing rate-limiting in the application logic itself. In addition, employing CAPTCHA system or user authentication can significantly help in distinguishing between human users and bots.

12.3. Scenario Three: Content Delivery Network

Next, consider a Content Delivery Network (CDN) that employs AWS WAF along with AWS Shield. The CDN has viewers around the globe who regularly access its content.

The WAF was set to block requests from certain countries to streamline content delivery to the target audience and to prevent potential geo-location based attacks. However, there were significant false positives, as legitimate users travelling in these blocked countries or using VPNs with those IP addresses were blocked from accessing the content.

The appropriate response was to adopt a more granular approach to filtering. Rather than blocking all traffic from certain IPs, the security team decided to use AWS WAF's GeoMatch feature, refining rules to block only specific types of requests from those IP addresses. Additionally, they implemented a user feedback mechanism to identify false positives and make necessary adjustments promptly.

Each scenario brings unique experiences to the table, offering an insight into real-world situations where AWS WAF and AWS Shield false positives need addressing. By understanding these scenarios, organizations can better navigate the complex labyrinth of false positives, leading to more secure and efficient operations. Remember, all these solutions should be augmented with a robust incident response mechanism. Having a team that understands these scenarios and is ready to react swiftly in case of a false positive is crucial to the overall integrity of your online presence. Always ensure your security strategies evolve with your organizational needs and emerging security trends.

Chapter 13. Building a More Secure Future: Best Practices and Recommendations

As you pave the way to a more secure future for your operations in the cloud, implementing best practices and acting on pertinent recommendations is essential. To help leverage the most of what AWS WAF and AWS Shield have to offer, here's a comprehensive guide that targets not only the reduction of false positives but also the bolstering of your overall security stance.

13.1. The Significance of Security Groups and ACLs

The groundwork for application security on AWS starts with Security Groups and Network Access Control lists (ACLs). Security groups act as firewalls for associated Amazon Elastic Compute Cloud (EC2) instances, controlling both inbound and outbound traffic at the instance level. ACLs, meanwhile, function as firewalls for controlling traffic in and out of a subnet within your VPC.

In essence, security groups regulate access to EC2 instances, while ACLs manage subnet traffic. Using these effectively can minimize threats and reduce the number of false positives.

13.2. Leveraging AWS WAF and AWS Shield Configurations

Understanding and configuring AWS WAF and AWS Shield is the next important step. AWS WAF provides customizable web security that protects your applications from common exploits, while AWS Shield delivers DDoS protection for applications running on AWS.

For AWS WAF, creating WebACLs (Access Control Lists) and corresponding conditions and rules can filter the traffic that reaches your applications. Strategies such as employing a "default deny" policy, limiting the rate of requests, and blocking known malicious IP addresses can strengthen your defenses.

To support AWS WAF configurations, AWS Shield Standard integrates seamless DDoS protections for all applications running on AWS. When facing larger, more sophisticated attacks, upgrading to AWS Shield Advanced provides cost-effective protection, with access to the AWS DDoS Response Team (DRT) and financial protection in the event of a DDoS attack.

13.3. The Power of Logging and Monitoring

Continuous logging and monitoring of your traffic and potential false positives are key to maintaining a strong security posture. AWS provides numerous tools to achieve this, including AWS CloudTrail and AWS CloudWatch.

CloudTrail lets you capture all API calls for your AWS WAF, Amazon EC2 instances, and many other services. By tracking each action, you can identify patterns, uncover violations, and rectify any issues.

CloudWatch gives an in-depth view of all your AWS resources, applications, and services running on AWS and on-premises environments, which aids in spotting trends, patterns, and potential issues.

13.4. Reduction of False Positives through Rule Tuning

Rule tuning is a potent method for reducing false positives. By auditing the impact of WAF rules against your logs regularly, you can refine these rules based on the screening results. If certain rules are triggering too many false positives, fine-tuning them will balance the security and traffic flow. Reviewing and improving rules should be an ongoing process, aiming to keep pace with evolving threat landscapes.

13.5. The Importance of Incident Response

Even with the best planning and practices, incidents can still happen. A clear, documented incident response plan that includes preparation, identification, containment, eradication, recovery, and lessons learned stages is important to minimize the impact of any security breaches.

13.6. Regular Security Assessments

Consistent security assessments provide a clear understanding of security risks and gaps. These assessments are not about scaring oneself; instead, it's about knowing and addressing vulnerabilities before they're exploited. Tools such as Amazon Inspector for automated security assessment services can help spot potential security weaknesses.

In the realm of AWS WAF and Shield, taking a proactive approach to your security and planning will only ever serve to benefit you. Taking the time to understand the workings of these services and how best to deploy them offers the most promising route to a robust security framework that can face false positives without causing disruption.

www.ingramcontent.com/pod-product-compliance
Lightning Source LLC
Chambersburg PA
CBHW061055050326
40690CB00012B/2635